# Cyberbullied by the Mean Girls!

## - A Quick Help Book for Tweens and Teens

The story in this book is a work of fiction. All incidents and dialogue, and all characters are products of the author's imagination and are not to be construed as real. All the characters, schools, buildings, streets, and events portrayed in this book are fictitious. Any similarity to real events, persons, buildings, streets, schools, or characters, living or dead, is coincidental and not intended by the author.

Copyright © 2012 A.T. Sorsa

All rights reserved.

ISBN-13: 978-1470019785
ISBN-10: 1470019787

## CONTENTS

FOREWORD .................................................... 1

1 CYBIL AND HER FOLLOWERS ........................... 8

2 CYBIL'S PLANS .......................................... 18

3 MELANIE – THE TARGET! ............................... 23

4 AFTER SCHOOL .......................................... 36

5 CYBERBULLIES IN ACTION ............................. 46

6 NO ACCESS ............................................... 50

7 CYBERBULLIED! .......................................... 52

8 HOW TO STOP THE CYBERBULLYING? ............. 63

9 CONCLUSIONS ........................................... 77

10 WHAT DID MELANIE DO RIGHT? ................... 87

ENDNOTES ................................................... 95

QUESTIONS .................................................. 98

TIPS ........................................................... 101

ABOUT THE AUTHOR ..................................... 105

BOOKS BY A.T. SORSA ................................... 107

# FOREWORD

Have you ever met any mean girls?
I bet you have. Maybe you are one of them or maybe you are one of their victims.

If you have met these mean girls then you know what they are like. You don't want to cross them. Not ever!

But these mean girls won't go away just because you wish that. You have to take your online life back from them.

Being bullied at school is bad, but being bullied online is even worse. You can't hide. You can only wish that they would stop the harassment! But how to do that? What can you do? Bullying can be stressing. It can harm you physically and emotionally.

Cyberbullying can be even worse than physical or emotional bullying, because cyberbullying can be done anonymously using technology, like for instance, cell phones and social network websites. Physical and emotional bullying happens usually in front of a limited audience – or when you are alone. Cyberbullying is for everyone to see online. You don't know who has read the messages or seen the pictures downloaded there by the cyberbullies. But you can be sure that the audience is more than just one or two – more likely all of your school friends are among the viewers, probably their friends, and the friends of their friends, too.

You might know the person/persons who are cyberbullying you, because usually they are someone you know and who know personal things about you. It would be harder for a stranger to figure out your password or your profile id.

Cyberbullying can include text messages, instant messages, emails, pictures, videos, or cruel or insensitive posts online. These messages can include personal issues that you would not like everyone to know. These messages and posts can contain claims about you or your life that are not even true.

Cyberbullying – just like physical or emotional bullying – happens frequently and more than one time. It is not just one time incident. It is done repeatedly.

This book tells you a fictional story of Cybil and Melanie. Cybil is the leader, the big cheese cyberbully, and one of the mean girls.

It deals with two difficult issues: cyberbullying and the bullying mean girls. Girls can be mean. But not just girls – all kids are capable of being cruel. Especially, when the kids are forming mini-societies at school – their own groups and societal levels with restrictions and rules. Some students are accepted in these elite groups and some not, some are being outcast and alone waiting to discover what they are great at.

What do you do when your school friends, the "rule setters," decide you're not cool? When and how do you get your parents involved without making things worse? Questions and tips how to prevent cyberbullying are included in this timely book about cyberbullying and mean girls.

This book shows some examples of what you can do if you are being bullied, what your parents and friends can do to help you.

However, this is book is not aimed to replace any professional help including teachers, school counselors, doctor, law enforcement, or even psychologist or psychiatrist.

All people are different, and they cope with difficult situations, bullying, and stress differently. Being cyberbullied is a nightmare, and the cyberbullied person need help, but you and your parents are the only ones who can decide what is best for you.

# 1 CYBIL AND HER FOLLOWERS

Cybil was very pretty and had always the newest clothes on. She was trendy. She was one of the most popular kids at school. She has a posse following her and mimicking her clothing, her hairstyle, and admiring everything she said.

Cybil thought she was perfect. She could not stand being around with other kids who were not as perfect, rich, pretty, or trendy as she was.

Cybil liked to pick on other kids, who were not as lucky or beautiful as she was. Usually Cybil just pointed out her victims to her closest followers, her posse, and her followers agreed on whatever she said and followed her example blindly. Their parents had not taught them good values. They were not taught really right from wrong or how to make the right choice of who to associate with. Cybil had a way of complimenting her posse so they liked to hear that and it made them feel popular and accepted.

The poor, bullied kids were usually embarrassed by Cybil's loud comments and acknowledgement that their jeans or blouse or shoes or earrings were not like hers, or not the latest trend anyway. They blushed, cried, or ran away. Nobody liked to be bullied and teased on the schoolyard. Nobody liked to be embarrassed. These kids usually looked afraid, timid, and did not seem to fit in with the other kids.

Cybil was good at emotional bullying. She did not have to use muscles to bully other students.

One day, there was a new girl attending the class. She did not look shy. She was pretty but she did not smile. Cybil noticed her when she entered the classroom.

Coyly touching her long, blond hair, Cybil turned to her posse, and said, "Look at her! Isn't she awful in that shirt? The color is so wrong, not this season."

They all stared at the new girl, who blushed. She knew she was being judged by the other girls. She could feel their eyes checking out every single detail on her outfit, her hair, and her appearance.

Actually, the blue colored shirt looked very nice on her, but Cybil's followers did not say that aloud. They wanted to please Cybil, their leader, not the new girl.

The teacher introduced the new girl, "This is Melanie Summers. She is new around here. Her family just moved here from Pennsylvania. Please, welcome Melanie."

"Melanie! What an awful name! So old-fashioned! Who would like to be called Melanie!" Cybil whispered aloud to her posse, barely audible.

They all giggled.

Her posse included four members: Diane, Brianna, Rose, and Sarah.

The teacher noticed the disrupting giggling and whispering and told Cybil and her followers to behave and be quiet.

Cybil smiled radiantly and said, "Yes, of course. My apologies."

Teacher's liked Cybil because she was pretty and she had a lovely smile. They believed she had potential to go very far in life. She was not the cleverest student in the classroom but she was doing average.

At lunch break, Cybil decided it was time to show who is the boss around here. When the new girl walked by, Cybil commented about her hair: "Who is cutting your hair… your dog? It looks shaggy!"

Cybil looked around and her followers laughed and repeat, "Yeah, who cut it?!" and giggled. They always did that. They wanted to be Cybil's friends and by inflating her ego, they did just that. Cybil was confident that she could say and do anything to any other student. She was not afraid of anyone or anything.

But Melanie, the new girl, was not laughing. She blushed and walked away to the farthest table so that she would not have to hear those comments again. It was emotionally challenging to start the new school and have no friends, but it was even worse to be sought out and be bullied the first day.

"Her clothes are so old fashioned," Cybil continued. "She probably gets them from a thrift store."

Melanie heard the comment and the giggles and echo of what Cybil said that followed it. She was upset, almost ready to cry. Flustered, Melanie tucked a wayward strand of hair behind an ear.

Melanie had thought that she looked just fine. She had taken time to choose the right clothes for the first day. She had chosen the light-colored capri pants and a light blue blouse, her long ash-blond hair coming to her mid-back. Defined black eyebrows, thick lips, and a delicate facial bone structure with dark green eyes gave the impression of a Barbie doll.

That was Melanie's only the first day at the new school.

Worse was coming…

If Cybil and her posse had come on that strong on the first day how was she going to be later in the year, Melanie wondered. She did not even know Cybil and her friends. Barely remembered their names after the introduction.

She did not understand why she was picked up and bullied the first day.

## 2 CYBIL'S PLANS

Cybil was bored at home. She had nothing else to do except to chat with her friends online and send instant messages. Then she got an idea! She could pretend to be Melanie's friend.

Cybil sent her a friend request and waited. She was sure Melanie would accept her request. She probably would not know who she was and would like to get new friends.

It took an hour before Melanie accepted her friend request.

Cybil sent IM to her posse informing that she was pretending to be Melanie's friend and they should follow her example.

Suddenly, Melanie noticed that she was very popular. Several girls had sent her friend request. Maybe the first day at school was not so bad. She did not know any of these girls.

Cybil asked her friends some ideas what could they do online to Melanie. She did not even think that she was going to be a cyberbully and her posse, too.

"We can try to steal her password and steal her account so that she can't get in!!" one of the girls suggested.

"Great! But it might take time to find out her password. We don't know her at all!" another posse member texted.

"Melanie probably has her pet's name as a password or something so stupid. LOL!!" Cybil replied.

"Then what can we do? :O)" Another posse member asked.

"OMG! Use your camera! Take some pictures of her and then modify the pictures!" Cybil said.

"I can follow her to chat rooms and post some messages on her blog if she has one…" another posse member replied. " Or on her website! Everyone uses one of the social network websites. She must have a profile in one of them!"

"LMAO! This is going to be fun! :O) !!!" Cybil replied.

Cybil's idea was actually a very bad idea. You don't want to harass or bully other kids just because you are bored and need some entertainment.

Now Cybil and her posse were all planning and sending IMs to each other all night long and giggling, thinking what fun it would be to harass this new girl online. And for what reason: just because Cybil was bored, and because she wanted to entertain herself, and because Melanie was the new kid with no friends. She was a potentially weak person with no peer protection.

## 3 MELANIE – THE TARGET!

Melanie was not aware that she was being targeted by the mean girls. She thought that the girls had been nice to her and decided to send her all the friend requests. She had accepted all the friend-requests the previous night.

Some girls had sent some comments of her pics online and sent some pics of the school. Everything seemed to be just fine.

Melanie had gone to bed thinking that the new school was not so bad if she could make this many friends the first day.

How wrong she was! She had no idea…

The next morning when she went to school, she was much happier than the previous day. She was waiting to meet the girls who had contacted her and asked to be her friend online.

Cybil and her posse were ready to take action.

One of the posse members, Brianna, had a cell phone with a camera. You know you are not supposed to have a cell phone at school, or not on during the classes, but this was early morning and they were all outside.

Brianna went to Melanie and asked, "Can I take a picture of you and then you and me together? I want to post it online….you know… to show everyone that we are friends now…"

Brianna was smiling, holding her cellphone-camera in front of her taking several pictures.

Rose joined her. She was also one of Cybil's followers. "Group pics are totally cool, aren't they?" Rose said to Brianna and winked. They both knew the real reason behind taking these pics. They needed the pics for tonight.

"Totally. Cooool!" Brianna said and giggled.

Melanie did not realize that something was wrong. She just thought that these girls were being nice to her.

Another posse member, Diane, went to Melanie and started chatting with her while they were walking towards the classroom. She said, "It is so hard to figure out good password. I always seem to forget mine. Do you know that I have to change my password every single time I log in because I can't remember it?"

Melanie thought she was either really lazy or unorganized. "Oh, but that's awful. I just use my cat's name and then my house number. It's easy to remember," Melanie replied without thinking that she just gave away valuable information that she would regret for the rest of the school year.

"Do you have a cat?" Brianna interrupted. "I love cats! They are so adorable! What's her name?"

"Queen."

"Queen?" Brianna asked.

"Yes, she is so queen-like, always so high and mighty, looks down on us humans," Melanie replied. "She is pure white and has blue eyes." "She loves to climb on top of our bookshelves or curtains or refrigerator," Melanie continued. "She likes to curl up with me during night time and then do long stretches with me when we woke up."

"OMG! Queen sounds so lovely!" Brianna and Diane replied.

Diane wrote down cat's name: Queen. Now they just needed to know her address to get the number for the password.

"Where do you live?" Brianna asked innocently.

"Oh, by the old cemetery. There was an old house that my parents bought when we moved here. It's quite big, and needs a lot of TLC, but otherwise it is okay," Melanie replied. "It has a tower in one corner, and the tower rooms are quite romantic. I like the old buildings with narrow windows and high ceilings," she added. "I don't mind that my parents are renovating it now. It's kind of nice to live there. It feels like the past is present when you live in an old house like that."

Melanie was enjoying her conversation with the girls. Maybe this school was not so bad, she thought.

"It sounds so cool," Brianna said. "Old building with a tower! You don't find many of those in this town."

"We need to hurry! The algebra class is about to start!" Brianna said and hurried inside the classroom and sat behind Cybil and winked her eye.

Cybil gave a quick, mean smile. Everything was ready for tonight: they would be able to attack Melanie's online account!

Melanie had no idea what these girls were planning. She was pleased to have found new friends.

Melanie was already thinking of inviting them over one evening after school to meet her family and her cat, Queen. Brianna and Diane seemed to be cat-lovers. She was sure they would love to meet Queen. They had asked questions about her pet cat, and they seemed genuinely interested in her cat and her life.

They would see the old building where they lived. They would also see what her parents planned to do with the interior decorator after the building was renovated.

Melanie loved the old building with the towers and lots of rooms. Most of the rooms were still unfinished, but the building itself looked like an old castle. Melanie thought that she was just like Rapunzel, a longhaired princess in a tower, waiting for her dream prince to arrive.

It would be fun to ask her new school friends for a pajama party! Her parents would be so happy to see that she had made friends so fast! Melanie thought and smiled.

But Melanie had no idea what these mean girls were planning.

Melanie had no idea what they could do…and how far they could go with her information. She thought she was just making friends with these girls, and there was nothing to worry about. Melanie trusted these girls too easily. She was too naive to even think that other girls would be so mean.

## 4 AFTER SCHOOL

That same day after school, Diane and Brianna rode their bikes by the old cemetery following Melanie and they learned where Melanie lived.

Melanie did not take the school bus. She lived quite close to school.

Brianna and Diane did not follow Melanie too close. They did not want Melanie to notice them and realize that they were following her.

But Melanie never looked back. She never noticed that she was being followed. She walked straight to home, and went inside the huge, castle-like building.

Melanie's new home was an old, redbrick building with a tower. There were lots of bushes around the building with tall  oak, maple, and willow trees.

Brianna took some pictures of the house and the street with her cell phone.

They saw Melanie's profile in one of the upstairs windows and they had to hide behind the trees so that she would not notice her "new friends" stalking her. But now Brianna and Diane also knew where Melanie's bedroom was. That might be useful information, too.

Brianna and Diane hurried back to meet Cybil. They had all agreed to meet at Cybil's after school.

The sun was setting toward the horizon, painting the street buildings near Cybil's house in red and gold shades. The dark clouds were gathering on the horizon. It was supposed to rain later that night.

The girls had planned to stay overnight with Cybil.

Cybil opened the door and smiled when she saw Brianna and Diane. "Hi, Rose and Sarah are already here," Cybil said and asked, "Did you get the address?"

"Yes, we know where she lives. We have the house number," Diane said and smiled.

Cybil looked pleased. These girls were great.

Diane and Brianna stepped inside and Cybil closed the door.

Cybil's parents were dining out so the girls could have some time alone.

"We also took some pics of the house." Brianna informed.

"And we know which one is her bedroom," Diane added.

"Really! OMG! That's so great!" Cybil said and a smile brightened her face.

They all giggled when they ran upstairs to Cybil's room. They were ready to start their harassment online.

"What do we do now?" Rose asked. She was not so sure that this was such a good idea to hack into Melanie's account online and harass her, but she wanted to be Cybil's friend. She liked to be one of the cool and popular girls.

Sarah was more interested in boys than the other girls, and she said, "There are more possibilities of damaging her 'good girl' reputation when we know her bedroom's location... and there is a tree conveniently right below it..."

Cybil opened her laptop. She had a pretty pink, brand new laptop.

Diane sat down by the laptop and started testing the website and what would be Melanie's correct password. It took her only a couple of minutes to find out the right combination of the cat name, Queen, and the house number 1234. "I got it! It's 1234Queen. We are in! We have access to her account!"

"OMG!" Cybil said and hugged Diane.

"Let's begin!" Cybil announced.

All the girls giggled in excitement. This was going to be fun.

The girls gathered on top of Cybil's bed and started planning what to write and post on Melanie's website. First, they decided to change her profile picture. Then they started editing the pictures Brianna and Diane had taken the same day.

Outside, it was already dark. It had started raining. All that was left was the falling rain, each raindrop making a soft tap as it landed against the roof and the window glass.

# 5 CYBERBULLIES IN ACTION

"Brianna, do you have your notebook with you?" Cybil asked.

"Yes, of course. I always have it with me," Brianna replied and pulled it out of her bag.

"Can you start editing the photos on your computer?" Cybil asked.

"Sure! No problem!" Brianna replied.

She downloaded Melanie's pictures on her notebook and opened a photo editor.

"Can you make her face rounder?" Cybil asked.

"You mean like this?" Brianna asked and made Melanie's face look like an oversized balloon.

All the girls laughed when they saw the new image. It looked awful.

"OMG! She looks like a pig!" Rose said.

"Moonface!" Sarah said.

"That's perfect!" Cybil said and wiped the tears of laughter. "Let's download it to her website."

"Diane, can you change the password on Melanie's account online?" Cybil asked.

"Done!" Diane said. "Now only we have the access! The new password is 5friends," she added.

"That's us!" Cybil confirmed.

They modified more pictures the same way. They also marked her bedroom on one of the house pictures, and wrote a comment on her website: "This is my bedroom. If you are looking for some fun, please visit ;) "

They also modified bikini pictures of Melanie by placing her face on a model's body, and then posted them online.

Cybil and her posse had so much fun thinking what Melanie would say when she notices that her account had been hijacked, and when she finds out what is going on there…

# 6 NO ACCESS

Melanie tried to login her online account. She got the message:

**"Incorrect password. The password or the login name does not match our records. Please try again."**

She tried several times with no luck.

She tried to change her password with no luck; somebody had changed the email address attached to her account. She had no access to her account. It was the same account that Cybil and her posse had accessed and were using modifying now.

She went to bed without any knowledge of what was going on online.

She did not even thought about the possibility that someone could have hacked into her account and stole it from her. She just thought that she miswrote something, and decided to give up and try again tomorrow.

# 7 CYBERBULLIED!

The next morning was windy. The rain had stopped and the streets were still wet.

When Melanie arrived to school, she noticed that the other students looked at her peculiarly.

What is going on, she wondered. They treated her like she had some contagious disease, she thought. Something must have happened yesterday or this morning. But what? She could not figure out what was wrong. She tried to remember if anything special happened the day before, but she could not think of anything that could cause this kind of reaction from the other students.

Melanie looked around and then she saw Brianna and Diane with Cybil. She decided to go and ask if they know what was going on. She walked across the schoolyard towards them.

"Hi, what's going on?" Melanie said.

"Awkward…" Cybil said to her group, and they all turned their backs on Melanie.

Melanie looked surprised. Her cheeks turned cherry red. She had no idea what was going on. She had thought that these girls were her friends now, but this morning they acted really strange.

The wind blew and shifted some stringy, long curls to block her eyes, and she pushed them back with a shaky hand. Something was off this morning.

Melanie walked towards the classroom when one of the other girls stopped her and asked, "Is this really you? Is this where you live? Did you post all this information on your website?" The girl looked at Melanie and held her tablet in front of her and waited for Melanie to answer.

Melanie looked puzzled.

"I don't know what you are talking about. I have a website, but I have not posted any pictures of my home there," Melanie replied.

"I'm Penny. You probably don't remember me, but I sat behind you in the homeroom," Penny said. "But anyway, there are some pictures online that you should see..." Penny added.

Melanie nodded. She was curious now to see what Penny was talking about.

"I think you're in trouble. Look at these pictures," Penny showed Melanie her table with online access.

"There is also a picture of your house with an arrow pointing to your bedroom. I guess you did not download that picture online yourself?" Penny said.

"No, show me," Melanie begged.

Penny showed a distorted profile picture that used to be Melanie and also an invitation for all the boys at school to come and visit her at her house. The picture showed her home and her bedroom. There was also an open invitation for all the kids to come to party at her house the same evening!

Melanie paled when she saw the picture and the text. She looked like a ghost of herself. Melanie browsed through her account, horrified of the distorted images of her, the picture of her house, and all the postings on her online account. She had no idea who could have done this. How could she delete these?

How could anybody know this? How could anybody do this to her? Melanie wondered. Her family just moved here. Nobody could possibly know where she lived. She had not invited anyone to her home yet, she thought.

"This can't be my account?!" Melanie said horrified. She could not believe her eyes. The pictures did not look like her, but they were still pictures of her. She recognized her clothes. She had worn them the day before when Brianna was taking the pictures... Brianna and Cybil? Could they have done this? Melanie wondered. She did not say it out loud. But who else could have done it, she thought.

"OMG! This can't be happening to me..." Melanie sighed.

This was a nightmare. What if my parents find out? Melanie thought. I have to tell them before they see this. I have to tell them I did not post these online, none of these.

"Do you know who posted these pictures and messages?" Penny asked. "You know you are being cyberbullied. You should tell your parents. You might get lots of calls and visits because of this," Penny informed Melanie. She saw how distressed Melanie was becoming.

Actually, Melanie was shocked. She still could not grasp that she was being harassed online. And why?

Melanie had not even thought about that someone would try to cyberbully her. Why would someone do that to her? She was a nice girl. The cyber bullying would be something that could happen to someone else and not to her. She was just a normal girl. Nothing special. No reason for anyone to cyberbully her.

Melanie could not deal with this and the looks of the other students. She was very embarrassed. She ran out of school and straight back to home. She did not want to talk to anyone or see anyone.

# 8 HOW TO STOP THE CYBERBULLYING?

Melanie had no idea what to do. She had no access to her online account. She could not take away the awful, distorted pictures of her. She could not undo any of the "invitations" online to visit her home. She was helpless.

The sky was cloudy. The wind was blowing the leaves along the sidewalk, and they were swirling in front of Melanie, when she ran back home. She banged on the door as if that would help everything to go away.

"Melanie! Why are you back so soon? Was there only a half day at school today?" her mother asked worried when she came out from the study to see who it was.

"No..." Melanie could not say anything else. She started crying and she ran upstairs to her room and threw herself on her bed.

Her mother followed her upstairs. "Melanie! Tell me what's wrong? Is someone being mean to you at school?"

Melanie's mother sat by her bedside in her dressing chair.

Melanie turned her head away.

"Melanie! Talk to me!" Melanie's mother insisted.

"Somebody hacked on my online account," Melanie sniffed. "They put some horrible pictures there of me. They wrote some fake invitations online... asking boys to visit my bedroom, and asking all the other students to come to party here tonight."

"But that just can't be true! We just move here. Who would do that to you?" her mother asked, worried for Melanie.

"I... I met some girls at school... I thought they were my friends. They took some pictures of me with their cell phone... I did not know they were going to be mean to me! I did not know they were going to use the pics this way!!" Melanie sobbed. Tears welled up in her eyes when she looked at her mother. Her mother held out her hands to pull her into a hug.

"Show me what they did," her mother asked.

"Okay… but I can't access my account. I think these girls have hacked into my account and changed my password..." Melanie said. She opened her computer to show her mother and showed her account pictures and all the messages. All the horrible pictures were still there as well as the fake invitations to visit her house tonight.

Her mother looked serious. "When was the last time you accessed your own account?"

Melanie said, her eyebrows bunching, "I think it was yesterday morning before school. I could not get into my account last night when I tried."

Melanie's mother raised her eyebrows as she browsed through the website and read everything that had been posted there since the previous day.

Melanie was still crying.

"Let's call your father and also the principal's office. Tell me the names of all the girls you think are behind this," her mother said with a serious voice.

"This is serious. These girls better learn that hacking and stealing somebody else's account is a crime. Also cyber bullying is a crime in this state," Melanie's mother said. She picked up the cell phone and called her husband and then made another call to Melanie's school.

"I will also call the police and inform them about the hacking and cyber bullying," Melanie's mother told Melanie. "This is not just a prank. They stole your account. They are sending messages online pretending to be you."

A police officer came within twenty minutes after Melanie's mother had called them about hacking and cyber bullying.

The police officer asked Melanie about the girls involved in this incident. Melanie replied, "I think their names are Cybil, Brianna, Rose, Sarah, and Diane. I don't know their last names. I just started school there."

"How did these girls found out where you lived? Clearly they know where you live because there is a picture of your home here with the sign to your bedroom," one of the police officers said.

Melanie bunched her eyebrows and thought about what to say. She was not sure. "I think they … or one of them… must have followed me home yesterday after school," Melanie said.

"Why do you think so?" the police officer asked.

"I recognize my clothes. I wore those yesterday," Melanie replied.

The police officer wrote a note about it.

"How do you think they found out where you live?" the police officer asked.

"I did not tell them my address, but I told them we live close to the old cemetery. I never told anyone where my bedroom is!" Melanie said.

"Then they are stalking you," the police officer replied and wrote a note in his small notebook. "They must have seen you going inside the building and then waited outside while you turned the lights on in your room."

"Oh, I see. That's possible. I usually always go to my room first," Melanie replied.

"How do you think they got access to your account?" the police officer asked.

"I did not give them my account number… unless…" Melanie remembered the conversation of the passwords… "One of the girls, I think it was Brianna, told me how difficult it was to remember all the passwords online and she said she always had to create a new one. She asked me how I remember my passwords…" Melanie blushed in anger. She had been so stupid! She had practically told them her password. "I told them I use my cat's name and our house number in my password…"

"So they followed you and got the house number. And you told them your cat's name?" the police officer asked.

"Yes, they asked if I had any pets. I told them about my cat Queen," Melanie replied.

Melanie remembered how she had told them about her cat and how cute she was.

"It was Brianna who asked about my cat and her name. I told her about my cat," Melanie said. She remembered now how they had pretended to be stupid and asked how she remembered her online passwords. She had told them.

Melanie got angry. She had been so stupid! How could she have not noticed what the girls were doing. They were fishing information from her. Brianna had been so good. And all those friend-requests online! She had thought that it was nice that all these girls wanted to be her friend, but instead they wanted to harass her online.

"So, it's all my fault. I gave them the information and they used it," Melanie summarized.

"No, definitely not. These girls are the cyber-bullies. They are the ones who hacked your account. They choose to hack into your account and pretend to be you online. You did not do that," the police officer replied. Then he turned to Melanie's mother and said, "We will contact the school and find out the last names of these girls, and then we will contact their parents. Hacking and cyber bullying are serious issues."

"We will keep our door closed tonight in case any of the other kids will try to come here and party. I think Melanie should sleep in another room tonight," Melanie's mother said.

"That's a good idea. Also, you should inform your website's administrator that somebody has hacked into your account and ask them to close it," the police officer advised. "We will send a patrol car around here after dark. That will keep the kids away, too."

# 9 CONCLUSIONS

The evening was kind of chaotic. Kids were dropping by to see the party house. Some boys were even trying to climb up the tree. However, they were interrupted by the police patrol. Melanie and her parents were allowed to be alone.

Cybil and her posse, Brianna, Rose, Sarah, and Diane, were reprimanded by the principal. They all got two weeks of out-of-school-suspension because of the hacking and cyberbullying. They also had to make up the lost time during summer school.

Even though their parents told the school and the police officers that "kids are just kids" and "it was just a prank, that's all" the mean girls were charged with criminal harassment and identity theft.

Identity theft was a serious issue because they had purposefully taken Melanie's password and hacked into her account online. These girls had stolen her identity online. They had written lies about her, and posted distorted pictures of her and falsified invitations to visit her home.

Melanie's parents were also concerned how the online information could be taken away. They were worried that those pictures and that information would follow Melanie for the rest of her life and create serious compromises in her career choices. No employer would like to hire a party-girl with pictures online. Nowadays the employers were so careful and they checked the social network websites to find out more about their employees. Melanie would soon look for her first job and now this cyberbullying could harm her future, too.

Cybil and her posse got away with the criminal harassment charges because this was the first time they had done it, and it was done only once. However, they had to go to juvenile court because of the identity theft and hacking.

Their parents were not pleased with the fact that their children were taken into the juvenile court. It seemed as if they had failed their duties as parents. They were embarrassed and angry. But Cybil and her posse were really embarrassed. They had never thought of that their hacking would be revealed and to be considered as a real crime. They had never thought of that they would have to go to court for criminal charges and that they would have a permanent record that would impact their work and career possibilities.

Internet and computer crimes are difficult and there are different laws involved. To catch Cybil and her posse who now were involved in cybercrimes, investigators relied on collection of evidence through computer and cell phone seizures to prove Melanie's harassment and hacking.

Melanie's internet provider was also helpful and assisted the investigators by providing the information from Melanie's hacked account.

Diane, Brianna, Rose, and Sarah blamed everything on Cybil. They said it was her plan, her initiative, and she started the cyber bullying. Their attorneys managed to get them just probation for a year, but Cybil got the hard time.

Cybil's attorney had informed her that the juvenile record could follow an individual for the rest of her life. They had told her, her posse, and her parents that any decision made when you are underage can also affect you later on in your life.

Cybil got two-year sentence, but she was able to get out earlier because of her good behavior.

But criminal charges were not the only thing that happened to Cybil and her posse: Melanie's parents filed a lawsuit against all Melanie's cyber bullies and their families for $500,000. They did not win their case. Not many families or victims of the cyberbullies have got any refund of their suffering. Cyberbullying and identity thefts are still quite new crimes and the law has hard time keeping up with the new technologies and what crimes people can do with the technologies available.

Melanie closed her account online and did not open a new online account for another year. She wasn't ready to be online and chat with anyone after this incident. It was scary to go back online. She had asked her mother to contact the webmaster and close her previous account permanently.

Melanie took back the time she would have used online to explore other interests. She got new hobbies, like for instance, painting, and dancing.

Melanie had nightmares after the incident. She did not like to go to this school with Cybil and her posse, and her parents decided that it is better if she changed to another school.

Penny stayed as her friend even if she moved to another school. She was the same girl who had told her about the harassment and hacking her online account.

Melanie's new school and new classmates had heard about the incident, but they treated her nicely. The incident had been in the news because Melanie and her parents had chosen to tell their story online. Cybil and her friends did not tell their side of the story. They chose not to comment anything to the news reporters. Because they were still underage their records were not public and the reporters could not access them.

Melanie was happy again: she had a new school, new friends, and Penny was still her best friend, and the best of all was the fact that the cyberbullies did not bother her any longer. She was now more careful when she opened an online account, chatted online, and invented her passwords. She never used her cat's name, or her address number on her password. She rather used random numbers, capital letters, and words that did not mean anything. They were more difficult to figure out.

## 10 WHAT DID MELANIE DO RIGHT?

If you are being cyberbullied, or physically or mentally bullied by someone, you need to consider what you can do to help yourself. Professionals or your parents can help you.

Keeping it inside you does not help. It will stress you, depress you, and make you sad, and you'll waste a lot of time by worrying and stressing alone while you could be doing something else, something fun.

Now in this story, there are some examples what you can do and what you can learn from this story when dealing with a group of bullies. These are discussed below in the following paragraphs.

**Find support**

Melanie found a new friend who helped her to cope with the cyberbullying situation even before the law enforcement got involved. A friend is always good to have.

**Find new friends and new hobbies**

She did not withdraw herself and avoid all the contacts because of some mean girls cyberbullied her, she allowed herself to find new friends by using her time with other interests.

## Don't let the bullies win

She did not let this unfortunate and nightmarish situation to put her down.

She did not let the bullies win. She stood up and fought back.

She informed the appropriate authorities and allowed them to do their job.

## Let your parents help you

She did not let herself to be alone in this cyberbullying situation. She let her mother help her. She let her be her ally and opened up to her. Adults have more experience in different social situations, and they have usually good instincts, let them help you if you being bullied!

Melanie's mother was ready to help her. It also made her feel good to be able to help her child.

That's what parents are for!

## Observe and ask yourself why

Melanie's mother was not at school when the situation started.

Maybe she would have noticed that something was going on with these mean girls, maybe not. But she might have been able to observe how these mean girls interacted and advised to steer clear from them and their behavior.

First day, this group did not want to be friends with Melanie, but suddenly, they changed their behavior.

If someone does that, be aware. Ask yourself: why do they want to be my friend now? What is the reason behind their actions?

**What your parents and your friends can do for you when you are being bullied**

Your parents can actively listen to your problems just like Melanie's mother did in this story.

Even if they don't have immediate answer, just telling what is going on and what is wrong in your social life, can help you. You'll share the burden! More brains working around the same problem is better than just one! Besides, often the person being bullied cannot find the way out by themselves. You need others to view your situation and find different solutions.

It is easier to come up with alternative activities to avoid the interaction with the bullies and bring around new opportunities.

**Professional help**

Your parents can help you to find professional help to solve a bullying situation. A professional help can include teachers, school counselor, the law enforcement, doctor, or even psychologist or psychiatrist. They can help you to self discover what you are good at. They can help you to deal with the stress, fear, and depression caused by (cyber)bullying.

Only you and your parents can decide what you need and what will be good for you in your situation because everyone is unique, and they deal with difficult issues in a different way – some take bullying harder than the others and some can find their own way how cope in diverse social situations.

**What else you can do yourself**

Don't repeat the same mistakes what Melanie did in this story: don't reveal your passwords to anyone.

If you know a cyberbully and his/her victims then inform authorities. Don't be quiet! Be an ally to this victim.

Keep on discovering about your interests and yourself. Your life is all about you.

Remember to thank your network – your friends, your parents, your siblings, your relatives, your teachers – for helping you out of the (cyber)bullying situation.

# ENDNOTES

If you are being cyberbullied by someone, then don't suffer quietly and alone.

You need to tell about the cyber bullying to your parents, your siblings, and your teachers. They can help you to contact the police, the parents of the cyber bullies, and help to stop the cyber bullying.

The cyber bullies will not continue for long, if you tell about them to an adult or to a police.

There are always consequences. Even if the teachers or parents talk to these cyber bullies, it might help. It does not have to involve the police or court. Sometimes, cyber bullying is hard to prove. In these cases, there might not be any criminal charges. Also, the parents and the school might want to keep the cyber bullying issue out of the courtroom and try to resolve the crisis by themselves. Sometimes, just a talk with the cyber bullies work; sometimes it requires the police and criminal charges.

Internet and computer crimes are not always easy to charge and to find solid evidence, and also different states and countries have different laws. It always depends on the case and what kind of cyber bullying has happened, how often, and how long time, and what kind of damage these cyber bullies have caused to the victim(s).

If you have ever planned or thought of harassing someone online, a word of advice: Don't! Cyberbullying and identity theft are serious issues. You will be in big trouble.

If you are a victim then tell the appropriate adult as discussed earlier. Then you must be very secretive about your identity and your personal information in all of your online activities. Always use the advised patterns of alphanumeric passwords when applicable.
Be safe.

# QUESTIONS

1. Have you ever been cyberbullied?

2. What did you do then? Who did you tell about the cyber bullying?

3. Has anyone ever hacked into your online account? What did you do then?

4. If your online account has never been hacked, what would you do if it happens?

5. What would you have done if you were cyberbullied like Melanie was?

6. Who would you have told about the hacking and cyberbullying?

7. Can you make a list of what are considered as cyberbullying?

8. Do you know anyone who is being cyberbullied or who has been cyberbullied before?

9. If you were cyberbullied, would you tell your teacher about it?
And if not, then why not?

10. If you were being cyberbullied, would you tell your parents or friends about it?

11. If you would not tell your parents about the cyberbullying, then why not?

12. Would you help someone else if you see him/her being cyberbullied? What could you do to help?

13. Why do you think the cyberbullies do what they do? What is their motivation?

# TIPS

The next list is for you to prevent cyberbullying to happen. Use it as a checklist when you are online and when you open an account online.

1. Don't post online any personal or sensitive information that you don't want everyone else to know.

2. Don't tell anyone what is your password.

3. Don't use the same password everywhere.

4. Use capital letters, small caps, and numbers in your password. It is more difficult to guess if it does not mean anything.

5. Don't use your pet's name, your sibling's name or your best friends name as password. Don't use your hobbies or interests in your passwords. These are easy to guess because you talk about these with your friends.

6. If someone is cyberbullying you online, don't answer his/her emails, instant messages and text messages. It will just make the cyberbully continue. Ignoring these messages and emails is better.

7. Don't delete the messages and emails that the cyberbully sends you. It is better to leave them

so that there is a proof that you are being cyberbullied, and that it has happened more than once. Also, it is easier to detect who the cyberbully can be if you keep the messages and emails.

8. Tell your parents about the cyberbullying. They can help.

9. Tell your friends about cyberbullying unless you suspect that they are doing it.

10. Friends can turn out to be cyberbullies. They know personal and detailed information about you. It is easier for a friend to guess your password because they know you. A stranger would have a hard time knowing or guessing your password.

11. Change your password often.

12. Don't harass, humiliate, embarrass, threat, or torment any other person online. You don't want to be a cyberbully.

13. If you know that someone is being cyberbullied, don't join the gang of cyberbullies. Be brave. Stand up for the cyberbullied! Help him/her. Tell about the cyberbullying to the teacher, your parents, and his/her parents. Cyberbullying can be stopped if you don't keep quiet and if you help.

14 "Do to others as you would like them to do to you." (Bible, Luke 6:31; Matthew 7:12)

# ABOUT THE AUTHOR

The author has written several quick help books for parents and children, and also illustrated children's books. The author has a PhD degree.

The author has had a lifelong interest in animals, writing, and drawing. She has a wealth of experience in the management area as well as social sciences. She holds a degree in marketing and management. She has since studied social sciences and has a particular interest in strategic management. She has gained experience in various consultancies and is now a freelance writer.

In her spare time, she can usually be found walking and drawing, but also enjoys evenings dining out with her family.

# BOOKS BY A.T. SORSA

*YA and Kids Fiction:*
Animellis Island Prequel: The Long Journey
Animellis Island Book One: The Traitor Gator
Animellis Island Book Two: Up, Up, and Away!
Animellis Island 2-book set
Mice and Owls
What is causing the scary nighttime sounds?
The Three Ghost Brothers
Instead of … Funny Rhymes Book One
Instead of… Funny Rhymes Book Two
Solo And The Bullybots – A children's book about bullying
My Name is Art – A children's book about bullying

*Quick Help Books for Kids, Tweens, and Teens:*
Time Management for Girls
Time Management for Boys
Bullies and Bullied
Cyberbullied by the mean girls!
Homar – The Homework Bully

*Quick Help Books for Parents:*
How to Motivate Your Kid – A Parents' Quick Help Book
Cyberbullied by the mean girls – A Parents' Quick Help Book